NITON PUBLISHING

JAGUAR

IN PICTURES

ROY BACON

First published in 1999 by Niton Publishing
P.O. Box 3, Ventnor, Isle of Wight, PO38 2AS

© Text copyright Roy Bacon 1999
© Photographs copyright National Motor Museum, Beaulieu, 1999

Acknowledgements
All photographs in this publication were supplied by the National Motor Museum, Beaulieu. Our thanks go to all the photographers who stood behind their cameras to record the history shown here.

A CIP catalogue record for this book is available from the British Library.

ISBN 1 85579 038 6

Design by : Roy Bacon and Joseph Murphy
Printed through World Print, Hong Kong

Title page : The wonderful XK engine that served Jaguar
so well in various forms.

Front cover: Postwar, the XK150, last of the XK line.

Rear cover: The prewar SS100 was the archetypal
British sports car.

JAGUAR
'Grace... Space... Pace'

The postwar advertisement said it all for Jaguar and the remarkable William Lyons who created the firm. His flair for style combined with a business sense that offered true value for money brought stunning cars that always stood out on the roads of the world.

First came Swallow Sidecars, making sidecar bodies in partnership with neighbour Bill Walmsley, and this led on to coach-building. By the late-1920s cars from Austin, Morris, Fiat and Swift with Swallow bodies were demonstrating the Lyons' line, but the important link was that with the Standard firm. At first the Standard Swallow was as the others, a new body on a stock chassis, but then came the SS1 with its short coupé body, long long bonnet, great looks and a low price. The concept ran from 1931 to 1936 in various forms to be joined that year by new SS sports models and the first of the Jaguar saloons.

The sports cars, the SS100 in two sizes, continued the theme of wonderful looks and a fine performance even if the handling needed respect. It all came at a price too low for the purists to accept, but the line became the archetypal sports car of the period. The saloons introduced the space element alongside the grace and pace of the line, and continued postwar in three engine sizes.

After the war the firm became Jaguar Cars and in 1948 launched the fabulous XK120 sports car with its wonderful six-cylinder engine having twin overhead camshafts that powered their cars into the 1980s. The XK120 typified Lyons' brilliance for it had such style and speed for its very modest price, while the engine soon found a second home in an improved saloon.

In the 1950s Jaguar went racing at Le Mans using the C-type version of the XK120 at first with wins in 1951 and 1953. This was followed by the D-type for 1954 and Le Mans wins in 1955, 1956 and 1957, both types built for sale in small numbers. The production model became the XK140 and then the XK150 while the big saloon was joined by a compact model, the Mk I, that was the start of another successful line that was raced on the circuits and much used in TV police series.

Then came the E-type in 1961 and once again Jaguar had produced a breath-taking sports car of tremendous performance and ridiculously low price. The saloons continued, some now with a Daimler badge for the 1960s saw the firm enmeshed with BMC and then Leyland. By then the saloon had developed into the XJ6 and by 1972 was joined by the XJ12 featuring a V-12 engine first used in the E-type.

The sports line became the XJ-S coupé in the mid-1970s as motoring became more refined and by 1980 Jaguar was its own company once more, although a decade later it became part of Ford. Before then it had returned, successfully, to sports car racing and Le Mans with some of this incorporated in the XJ220 concept car.

There was a new version of the old XK engine in the 1980s and this plus the V-12 carried the firm on. The style was amended but never by enough to lose the Jaguar line so that now, as then, the cars stand out from the crowd. In 1992 the XJ220 went into production, as stylish and as advanced as the cars that had preceded it.

For 1999 the S-type brought the compact Jaguar model back to the range with a dramatic debut at the British Motor Show. It was new, but the Bill Lyons style was still within its lines just as it had been right from the early days of the SS1 and later with the XK range and the E-type.

Seventy years of progress from the 1922 Swallow sidecar attached to a Douglas flat-twin of the period to the 1992 XJ220. Then, it was two or three speeds and either chain or belt final drive with magneto ignition, minimal brakes and no rear suspension. In that time motorcycles outnumbered cars on the roads, but everything would change by the time the XJ220 arrived.

Bill Lyons built special Swallow bodies for several marques from 1927 including this 1931 Wolseley Hornet. That model had a good six-cylinder, overhead-camshaft engine, but a weak chassis, so the improved style made it a good promenade sports car.

First of the Swallow conversions was to the Austin Seven in 1927. Underneath were stock components but Lyons transformed the looks in saloon, sports and coupé forms. The saloons often had the pen-nib, two-tone colour style, as on this 1931 model, and the ship ventilators were another neat touch.

Lyons built Swallow bodies for Morris, Fiat and Swift as well as Austin and Wolseley, but more important was his link to Standard. This 1933 picture shows the stock Little Nine Standard model on the left and the SSII that used its engine and chassis on the right with other models of the year to the rear.

Late in 1931 the SS1 coupé went on sale combining the side-valve, six-cylinder Standard engine with a chassis made by Standard for Lyons. On this went a small, two-door coupé body, close-coupled to seat four if two were midgets, behind a long, long bonnet. Dubbed the 'cad's car', it had the looks of expense but a low sales price ticket.

An English setting for an SSII of 1935 with the two-door saloon body. First seen in 1932 the model lost something of the style in being shorter, while its modest 1005cc side-valve, four-cylinder engine from the Standard Little Nine offered but a limited performance and improvement was ruled out by it having but two main bearings. It was revised from 1934 with a longer wheelbase, four speeds, better brakes and larger engines of 1343 or 1608cc, albeit still with side valves.

The SS1 was an instant success for it embodied Bill Lyons' precepts of simplicity, good design, style and a very competitive price. Under the bonnet went a 2054cc engine with 2552cc an option.

Part of Bill Lyons' success came from leaving what was right alone. This 1934 SS1 had gained flowing wings and running boards plus enough inside room to really be a four-seater in saloon or coupé form. The engine had an alloy head but the looks remained much faster than the power that continued to match the price.

Introduced for 1935 with a style to enclose the external trunk within the body, this Airline SS1 saloon has lost its spare wheel cover and a section of the running board that normally swept between the wings. Turn signals in these have replaced the semaphore arms that went just aft of the door hinges and the badge bar carries extra lights. Out front is the extension for that most useful of tools, a starting handle that can aid servicing as well as start the engine.

For the 1934 SS1 the frame was revised to give a wider track and more foot space in the front while engine sizes increased to 2143cc and 2663cc, and synchromesh appeared in the gearbox. Style for minimal money.

This 1934 SS1 tourer still had the side-valve engine, but enlarged, and an improved chassis so continued to offer the sports car line and a reasonable performance at a low price. This one moved to Europe and gained a second pair of horns and the central spot lamp, while the external wiper linkage and wire wheels on knock-off hubs were usual, but the side lamps were from an Airline saloon.

The SS90 was only built for one year, in 1935, and usually had the long flowing wings of the series, but this example has been altered to suit the rallies and trials its owner enjoyed competing in. The hat and coat hung on the gate most likely belonged to an observer positioned to check how the car coped with the road surface, gradient and corner.

Taken at an SS car club rally on a damp day, with a 1934 SS1 coupé in the foreground on the left and a 1935 Airline saloon beside it, the latter showing off its twin spare wheels and their covers. Another Airline is parked further back in a fine array of these desirable SS cars.

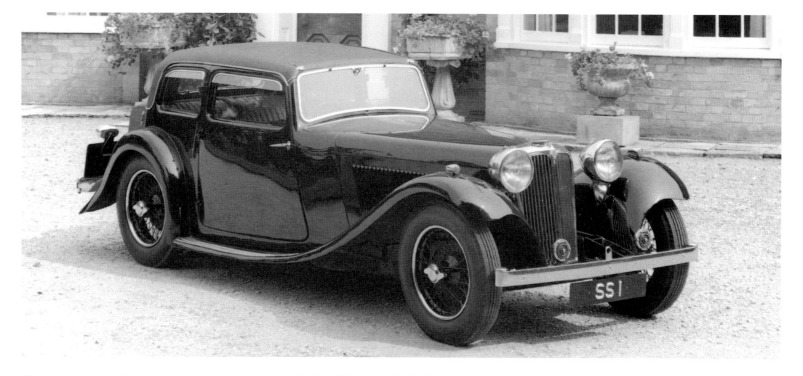

The two-door, four-seater saloon version of the SS1 for 1934 that had a line that would run on to the postwar Jaguar models for many years. All part of the Lyons' philosophy of getting it right and then leaving it alone. Graceful, although still cramped in the back.

Postwar, and still going strong in the 1954 Eastbourne Rally held in June that year, this SS tourer is in the middle of a special test involving a reversing manoeuvre. The good steering lock was an asset.

This 1935 SS1 drop-head coupé found its way to California and enjoyed the sunshine of the West Coast of the USA. A car well suited to that climate and life style.

Side view of a 1935 SSII saloon that shows how the shorter bonnet, compared to the SS1, detracted from the style and left the car looking much as others of the time. This, plus nothing special as to performance, limited sales as the competition was as good or better.

SSII CHASSIS SPECIFICATION

The bare chassis for the 1935 SSII that was strong, simple and cheap to build. Twin carburettors were standard with a single plus lower compression ratio the option. Four speeds, with synchromesh on three of them, Bendix brakes, Hartford friction dampers and Rudge-Whitworth centre lock wheels with 18-inch rims carrying Dunlop tyres made for a good specification.

Right: Brooklands in March 1939 and a 1935 SSII tourer undergoing a special test set out on the Campbell Straight where it ran alongside the Finishing Straight with the Members Banking in the background. The meeting was a Members Rally, organised by the Junior Car Club.

The full title for the ultimate prewar sports two-seater was Jaguar 2½-litre SS100 and 1936 the first year that the future company name was used. For most people SS100 was quite sufficient for this model that was taking part in the Scottish Rally and refuelling with Esso High Test at 1/8d for the gallon, a whole 2d more than plain Esso.

Taken in November 1934, this picture shows a long line of SS1 cars destined for export to America with an Airline saloon at its head. Some 600 of this then new model were built over two years, with most in 1935, so the Airline was not as popular as the firm had hoped, rather as Bill Lyons had predicted.

In the workshop, a 1936 Jaguar tourer with the 2¹/2-litre engine looks ready to go. Extra lamps at the front plus another fitted to the windscreen frame and discreet turn signals in the scuttle sides all add up to a car that is well looked after and much appreciated for what it is and what it can do.

THE 2½ LITRE JAGUAR OPEN TOURER

The first use of the Jaguar name came in 1936 for a new series of models that included this open four-seater tourer and a four-door saloon. The 2 1/2-litre car had a 2663cc six-cylinder, overhead-valve engine using the Standard seven-bearing bottom half and twin carburettors that drove a four-speed gearbox, all mounted in a new underslung frame. On this went the elegant bodies and the result was an excellent and stylish carriage.

The saloon version of the 2 1/2-litre Jaguar showed the classic marque lines to their best and should be compared with the earlier models to see how far and quickly Bill Lyons advanced. This fine specimen was taking part in the MCC Torquay Rally in prewar days.

This 1937 2¹/2-litre SS100 raised some dust while taking part in the 1952 Morecambe Rally held in May that year. A well preserved specimen that caught the eye of all watching with its fine lines, appreciated as always.

Same SS100 about to move off during the 1952 London Rally held in September, the driver A.R. Eastwood and the weather colder with a stiff breeze compared with the May event. Time for the heavy outer coat but the flat hat remained the same.

Winter in the early-1960s with the hood down but who cares when you have a 1937 2^1/2-litre SS100 to enjoy. Then, such cars were simply for motoring pleasure with the fresh air and better performance than a small saloon offered. Only later did they become collectable.

The new Jaguar range for 1936 included a 1½-litre model only built as a saloon and fitted with the 1608cc side-valve Standard engine from the SSII. However, it had a new frame, shorter than that of the 2½-litre model, and the same great Lyons style that would run for so long. It was somewhat heavy for the available power but still ran better than many others of the same capacity.

The SS team for the 1937 Welsh Rally lined up in their 2½-litre SS100 cars. Such events were popular in prewar days and cars in standard trim could run in them without serious damage while the rally would close with a social evening.

The SS100 title was adopted by the 3½-litre version when it appeared so applied to both capacities without distinction. Both were quick, cheap and had the archetypal 1930s sports car style of low build, flowing wings, cutaway doors and slab fuel tank at the rear. It irked the purists but gave real performance in either size. This one is taking part in a 1977 rally on a cool day, hence the raised hood.

Taken at Brooklands, this 2½-litre Jaguar saloon has just completed an event during an MCC meeting held at the track. It is at the Fork Finish where cars had to run past the Vickers Aeroplane sheds on a reverse curve between the two major bankings of the Outer Circuit.

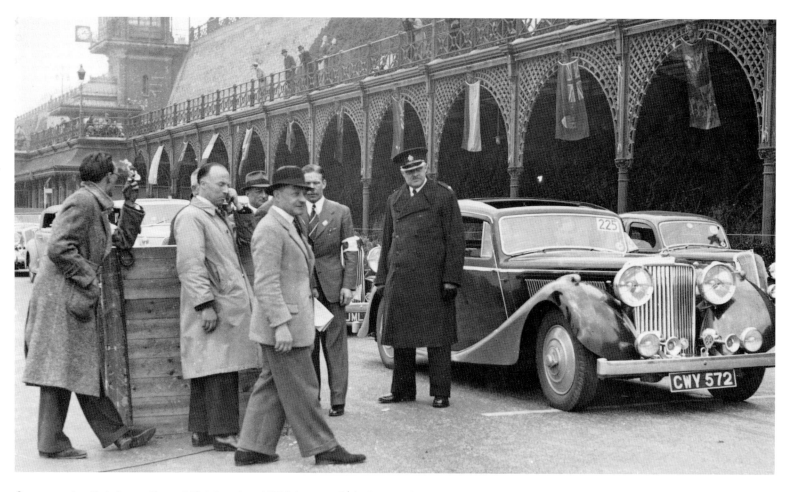

Seen at the Brighton Speed Trials, this 1938 Jaguar 3¹/2-litre saloon stands at the front on the line ready to go down the timed kilometer as fast as it can. The police kept an eye on proceedings while the man with the telephone checks that all is clear for the run. Wire connections were needed then, now there are other means.

Another point during the 1937 Morecambe Rally, one of several such annual events run by the MCC for cars and motor-cycles, with the 2¹/2-litre Jaguar saloon involved in a special test under watchful eyes. Tyre marks on the road show that others have already had their turn.

Taking part in a Scottish Rally, this 1938 SS100 is negotiating the Kenmore section with Loch Tay in the distance behind it. A fine way to see the sights of the country and the shadows and dust suggest a fine day for it.

Frontal aspect of the 1938 SS100 with its two large headlights, twin horns and fold-flat windscreen. Just over 300 of these cars were built with around 200 of 2^1/2-litre and the rest with the 3^1/2-litre engine. This one is as seen in 1967.

Dashboard of the 1938 3^1/2-litre SS100 with a well scattered array of dials, some carrying the 'SS' logo, plus the switches. Three levers on the steering wheel hub, aero screen for the driver alone, simple door catches, fire extinguisher and a spare inner tube in the passenger footwell. A 120 mph speedometer was necessary, and the rev-counter with in-built clock useful.

The Tower tells us it is Blackpool, as do the badges and pennants, and here the cars are lined up on the front at the end of their long drive during the rally. In the foreground is a 1937 Jaguar 2^1/2-litre saloon, known to its owner as the 'Grey Ghost' while beside it stands an Alvis.

A fine 3^1/2-litre SS100 parked outside the works showing off the detail points that endeared it to its owners and gave it style without excess cost. The jaguar on the radiator cap, wire mesh screens in front of both headlights and spot lights, the logo on the wheel nuts and twin aeroscreens all made their point.

The 3¹/2-litre Jaguar drop-head coupé made an excellent tourer with its smooth running engine and ample space for four. Underneath went a fine chassis while the Jaguar style was seldom bettered.

Showing no sign of its age, this 1939 Jaguar hustles round Goodwood during a BARC meeting in 1954. Could have either size of the six-cylinder engine under the bonnet and not hanging about. Then a cheap way to go racing but now a classic to be preserved and shown, in part due to its value.

In 1938 the spare wheel was moved from the front wing and a 3½-litre model joined the smaller cars, being offered as a four-door saloon, as here, or as a drop-head coupé. The engine was a 3485cc version of the overhead-valve six and the style was as good as ever. This example is taking part in a 1956 rally.

In October 1938 the firm showed this 3½-litre SS100 coupé at the London Motor Show held at Earls Court. Only the one was built as they concentrated on their existing range, but the line of the rear of the car found its way onto the postwar XK120.

Outside the works in 1939 with the 3¹/2-litre saloon whose line would continue postwar for some years. Then, the SS initials were dropped for they had become far from popular, and from 1945 the firm was known as Jaguar Cars Ltd.

Best of the prewar bunch, the 3½-litre SS100 from 1938 in all its glory and showing the skill of Bill Lyons in achieving such lines allied to a top speed over 100 mph, something few cars could reach then, all at a price far below that of his opposition. Wonderful and here seen restored in 1967.

This 3½-litre SS100 was built in 1946 to the proposed 1940 specification for Ian Appleyard to drive in the early post-war rallies. Here it is seen in 1965 following restoration to pristine condition.

Ian Appleyard and his co-driver Dr. Dick Weatherhead after the first postwar Alpine Rally held in 1947 which they won. The car was built in 1946, to the specification that would have been used for the 1940 models, and a fine array of awards stand on the bonnet to testify to Ian's skills.

Three-quarter rear view of a 1948 3¹/2-litre drop-head coupé standing outside a Rolls-Royce showroom. It continued to use the prewar 3485cc six-cylinder, overhead-valve engine and was also built as a saloon, both versions elegant on their wire wheels. Fast cars, but thirsty with heavy brakes.

The 1¹/2-litre saloon was shorter in the body than the larger capacity models and sold well fitted with the 1776cc four-cylinder, overhead-valve engine derived from the old Standard four. Not fast but well appointed and stylish.

This 1948 2¹/2-litre Jaguar took part in the 1953 Daily Express National Rally and is seen here during a special test held on the front at a seaside town.

ADVANCE PARTICULARS

OF THE NEW

JAGUAR

Type XK

"100" AND "120" SUPER SPORTS MODELS

FITTED WITH TWIN OVERHEAD CAMSHAFT ENGINES OF 2 LITRE OR 3½ LITRE CAPACITY

Jaguar issued this folder at the 1948 London Motor Show to introduce the XK120. The '100' model was never to reach the public and was a proposed version with a 2-litre four-cylinder engine with the same valve gear and other details as the six.

The big saloon became the Mk V for 1949 in 2½- and 3½-litre sizes, the changes including independent front suspension, using torsion bars, and hydraulic brakes. This batch of ten being hoisted aboard are due for a sea voyage in the forward hold, leaving from Southampton Docks.

Taken from the brochure given out at the 1948 London Motor Show, the page that introduced the XK120. In austere, postwar Britain where wartime restrictions were rife, petrol was still rationed and most cars much as prewar, it was the sensation of the show and soon proved that it had go as well as show.

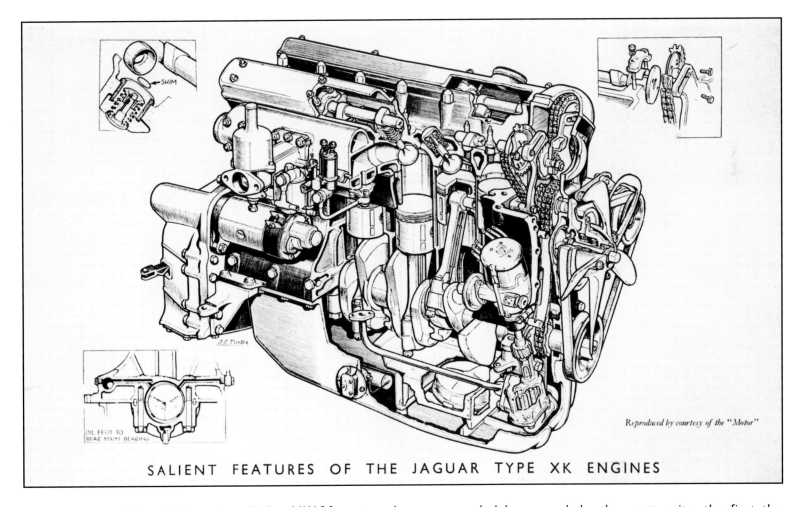

SALIENT FEATURES OF THE JAGUAR TYPE XK ENGINES

Line drawing of the 3441cc six-cylinder XK120 engine. It was preceded by several development units, the first the 1361cc XF four-cylinder whose twin-overhead camshafts were driven by a system much as that finally used. A single chain was also tried but had a high-pitched whine that could not be cured. Then came the 1775cc XG four with overhead valves and valve gear similar to that of the BMW 328, the 1995cc twin-cam XJ four and 3181cc XJ six.

Seen in 1949 at a corner of the Scarborough road racing circuit, an early XK120 of which the first batch had aluminium bodies because the car was intended for limited production as a carrier for the new engine and possibly some publicity. The flood of orders demanded a change to pressed steel and one effect was that the side lights were no longer separate items.

The Jaguar stand at the 1950 New York Show with the XK120 centre stage, a second example beside it, and three of the Mk V saloons for which the twin-cam engine was intended but not fitted.

132·6 M.P.H. ON PUMP PETROL · · · · ·

On May 30th, 1949, an entirely standard Jaguar 3½ litre XK 120 Sports Two-Seater, running on pump fuel, attained a speed of 132.6 m.p.h. over a flying mile on the Jabbeke-Aeltre Road in Belgium. This speed was officially timed by the Royal Automobile Club of Belgium and is the fastest ever recorded by a standard production unsupercharged car.

An advertisement put out by the firm to highlight the timed run of the XK120 on the Jabbeke-Aeltre Road in Belgium on May 30th, 1949, when it achieved 132.6 mph over a flying mile. For this it had the optional aeroscreen and undertray.

For 1949 the big saloon and drop-head coupé models took on the Mk V form that shared independent front suspension by torsion bars with the XK120. There were hydraulic brakes but the cars continued with the overhead-valve six engines of 2664 and 3485cc, and the line that ran back to prewar days.

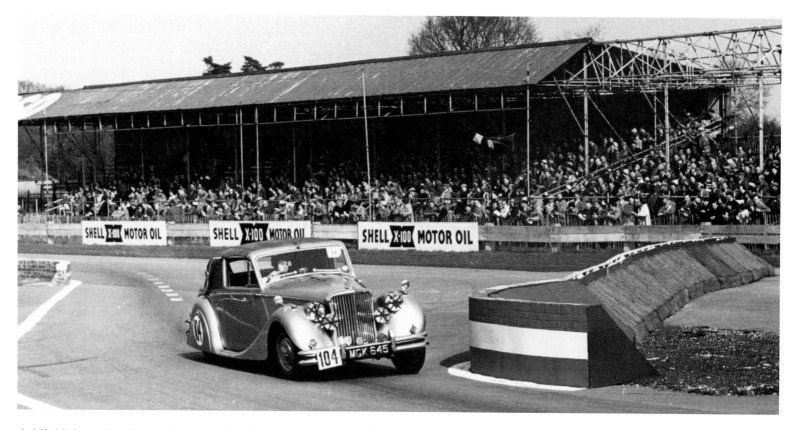

A Mk V drop-head coupé taking the chicane during a race at Goodwood held in 1954. The angle of roll indicates that the driver is pushing it to its limit which was as much as could be expected for such a car.

The XK120 was soon involved in competition and a trio of them are here starting in the 1950 Tourist Trophy race held at the Dundrod circuit in Ireland. Leslie Johnson has got his white car away first while none of the Jaguars should be troubled by the Austin A90 on the right. Stirling Moss won with Peter Whitehead second and Johnson third to make it a clean sweep for the firm.

Leslie Johnson took his XK120 to Montlhéry in October 1950 and he and Stirling Moss covered 2579 miles in 24 hours at an average speed of 107.46 mph to demonstrate its abilities. The final hour was completed at an average of 112.4 mph.

View under the XK120 bonnet where the top of the twin-cam engine and the two SU carburettors that fed it can be seen. It was a remarkable design by William Heynes, Jaguar Chief Engineer and Director, and would remain in use for some forty years in most of their cars in one form and size or another.

This 1950 Mk V is taking part in an event at Silverstone, possibly an MCC High Speed Trial where competitors had to cover a set number of laps in the time allowed for their award. Thus, not a race as such although it was hard to believe that when watching the cars going round.

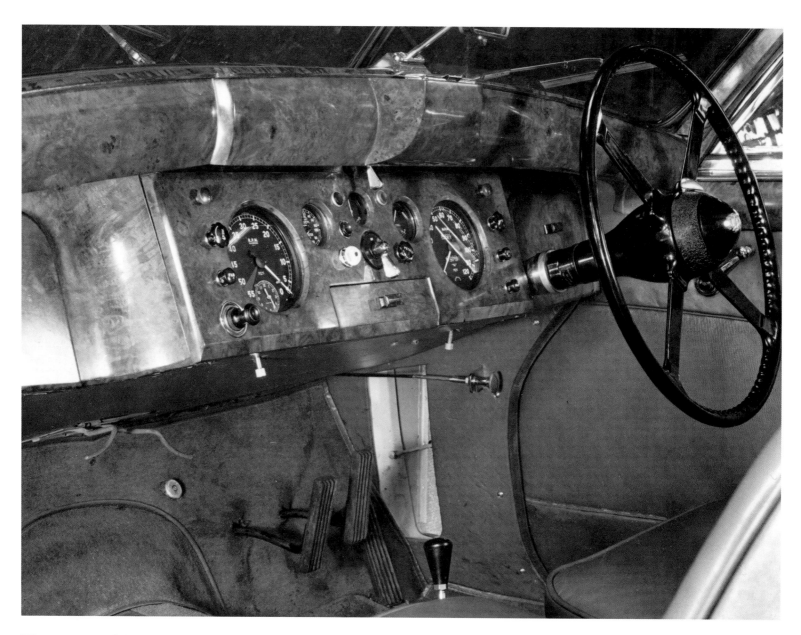

The interior of the Mk VII that appeared for 1951 to replace the older saloon. It was well appointed and finished by the standards of the time but to modern eyes seems dated. Note how the speedometer and rev-counter contra-rotate, not good instrumentation, and the second sits in front of the passenger although of more use to the driver. The steering column did not collapse on impact in those days so front end collisions were painful.

Line of Mk VII saloons at the International Trophy race meeting held at Silverstone in August 1955. At the start drivers would run to their car, leap in, hit the button and be off to the first corner. Under the bonnets went the 3441cc twin-cam engine from the XK120 which helped to move them all along.

The faithful overhead-valve engine of the Mk V that had served the firm well postwar and prewar where its roots lay in the 2 1/2-litre of 1936 and then the 3 1/2-litre of 1938. This was the larger engine final form with its twin SU carburettors and the graph related to the acceleration of the car.

Fine line of the 1950 Mk V saloon with its rear wheel spats and both doors hinged from their centre. Both head and side lights were blended into the front wings and the bonnet sides lost their louvres. A fine car with ample performance, especially from this 3¹/2-litre version.

An XK120 at the finish of a race with another close behind. The front bumper and number plate have been removed but not the extra lights while bonnet straps and a single aeroscreen have been added.

A fixed-head coupé version of the XK120 appeared for 1951 and continued the fine line although space for the two occupants was limited. Most in this form were built for export so the right-hand drive model was rare.

Rear quarter of the XK120 when amended for racing and fitted with the optional wire wheels held in place by two-eared knock-off hub nuts. The fuel tank was a further option, along with an auxiliary tank, and had an external, quick-release filler cap in place of the normal filler and its flush, hinged cap.

A 1951 XK120 Open Two Seater Super Sports car out in California where it was simply known as a Roadster and proved most popular. The simple, uncluttered line was thought the best by many owners.

Start of the sports car race held during the 1951 BRDC International Trophy meeting held at Silverstone and supported by the Daily Express. The field was dominated by XK120 Jaguars and at the finish they occupied the first five places with Stirling Moss the winner.

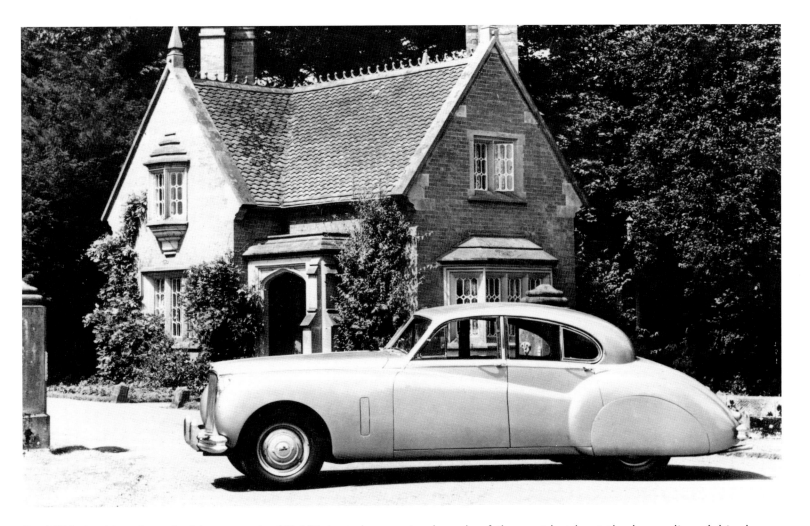

By 1951 the big saloon had become the Mk VII, lost the running boards of the past but kept the Jaguar line. A big, heavy and thirsty car that needed its twin-cam engine to propel it, but it was fast and handled well for its day and weight.

A fine pair of XK120 Roadsters taking part in the 1952 Morecambe Rally and about to run in a special test on the sea front. Lancaster, from where the organiser's caravan hailed, lies a few miles inland from Morecambe.

Lt.Col. Goldie Gardner was best known for his record breaking exploits using MG cars that included one run with a Jaguar 1995cc twin-cam XJ engine fitted. This had a 12:1 compression ratio and produced 146 bhp at 6,000 rpm, being safe to 6,500 rpm, and propelled his highly streamlined car to 176.6 mph over the flying kilometer in 1948 to take the class E record. He also drove Jaguar cars and this 1951 XK120 Roadster was one such.

The XK120 Roadster parked in Bakersfield, a Californian town located 80 miles inland from the coast and 100 miles north of Los Angeles. Good country for an open sports car with main highways for cruising and mountains close by for driving, while the wide roads made for easy parking. No doubt more congested now and the American cars much changed, but the Jaguar line was timeless and would still draw attention.

Luggage and clubs for a weekend break for four using a Mk VII to carry them to their hotel and the golf links. Matched cases for the boot to swallow and again typical of their time with two catches but no all-round zips.

Stately gates being serviced, hence the step ladder, with this work interrupted for the XK120 to have its picture taken. A fine car by a fine drive leading to a fine house.

Jaguar ran three XK120 cars at Le Mans in 1950 with one running third at the 20-hour mark when clutch slip put it out. They returned in 1951 with the XK120C when Peter Walker and Peter Whitehead won and Stirling Moss set the fastest lap, a record, before retiring when leading around midnight.

In the paddock prior to the 1951 Tourist Trophy race held on the Dundrod circuit in Ireland. Stirling Moss won and Peter Walker was second in car number 8 while number 9 was fourth driven by Leslie Johnson and Tony Rolt.

A Mk V Jaguar saloon taking part in one of the special tests at the end of the 1951 Monte Carlo Rally and not hanging around if the roll angle is anything to judge by.

The highly streamlined MG used by Goldie Gardner for several of his successful record breaking attempts. It ran well in Germany in 1939, and postwar with various engines including the 1995cc XJ four seen here in 1948. The engine was fitted with high-compression pistons for this task, in which it succeeded, and was the true forerunner of the long-running XK twin-cam six.

Well known XK120 used by Ian and Pat Appleyard in many rallies including this 1951 Alpine Rally. It took over from the SS100 built for Ian in 1946 and he was most successful in this type of event and associated with Jaguar for many years. In 1952 he was awarded an Alpine Gold Cup for wining Alpine Cups for three successive years, not an easy task.

Seen in 1979, a 1950 XK120 Roadster that had retained the separate side lights of the early cars and lacked the simple ventilator flap that came late in 1951 to allow fresh air to be drawn into the footwells. A happy family crammed into the two seats.

Waiting on the start line during the 1952 Brighton Speed Trials held over the standing-start kilometer, W.C.N. Grant is poised to unleash his XK120. Behind stand two more, one minus front bumper, while an official has an expression to suggest a hold up in proceedings.

All clear and the clutch had just gone home to hurl the Jaguar forward from the line while the timing hockey stick was withdrawn before the rear wheel had a chance to run over it. A fine September day brought out the spectators who had a good view from above or could mingle in the paddock.

A fixed-head coupé XK120 running in the 1953 RAC Rally held in late March. The weather looks cold, chilly and damp with the onlookers well wrapped up against the elements.

This 1952 Mk VII was fitted with a two-door coupé body by Pinin Farina but in the process lost most of the Jaguar style without adding the flair that the Italian house was famous for. Sad in view of the effort involved.

Stirling Moss takes his C-type Jaguar through the chicane at Goodwood during the 9-hour sports car race that ran from 3pm to midnight in 1952. His car took the class win and had led prior to a long pit stop to replace a suspension member.

In 1952 Jaguar took an XK120 to Montlhéry and ran it at 100 mph for seven days and nights. The drivers were Leslie Johnson, Stirling Moss, Jack Fairman and Bert Hadley and in all they covered 16,852 miles at an average of 100.31 mph to set four new World and five International Class Records.

The C-type driven in the 1952 Le Mans race by Peter Whitehead and Ian Stewart when all three of the team cars went out within three hours of the start. All suffered from overheating brought on by changes to the front end of the body and a repositioned radiator header tank.

The XK120 fixed-head coupé used by Leslie Johnson's team at Montlhéry in 1952 when they ran at over 100 mph for 100 hours and continued on for a further 68 hours to complete the seven days. After two days a back spring broke which cost them four hours to fix after Johnson had driven for nine hours with the broken spring, refusing to risk his co-drivers.

Lt.Col. Goldie Gardner and his wife with their Mk VII saloon at the 1952 Eastbourne Midnight Concours. Very much a black tie and evening dress affair with each car presented to the judges and the passenger attired to suit the occasion.

The engine room of Gardner's Mk VII with the same degree of shine under the bonnet as on the outside of the body. Much time and trouble had been expended to reach this level and more was required to maintain it.

Gardner's Mk VII in 1953 after the Brighton Coronation Concours d'Elegance with its award and the team that kept the car in its mint condition. Not an easy task even if the car was only used on fine days.

Interior of the Gardner Mk VII which was just as neat and tidy as the outside. The odometer indicates that the car has run for several thousand miles at least which makes its class win all the more worthy.

Goodwood in Sussex in July 1956 with an XK120 fixed-head coupé entering the chicane. The car had the Special Equipment option that included a camshaft with more lift, special crankshaft damper, lighter flywheel, stiffer springs front and rear, and wire wheels on knock-off hubs.

During the 1952 Goodwood 9-hour race Peter Whitehead crashed his C-type at Madgwick but was unhurt although the car was too damaged to continue and a spectator was injured. The straw bales and other barriers were typical of the time and a far cry from today's gravel traps.

A fine 1952 XK120 as seen in 1973. It has the separate side lights of the early cars but also the footwell ventilators, just ahead of the door, introduced from November 1951. Sleek lines of a classic that never dated.

The cockpit area of a left-hand drive XK120 Roadster of 1952 at a motor show with a coupé beside it and two Fords across the aisle. A fly-off handbrake was fitted, then essential wear for a sports car but now a distant memory.

The long-distance XK120 coupé on show in France with its measurements converted to approximate metric. Actual figures were 161.4 km.heure and 27,120 km, but either way it was a long way and a great achievement.

It was not until 1953 that a drop-head coupé XK120 joined the other two versions so it was only listed for two seasons and the car remained a two-seater. When folded, the hood went behind the seats but was not concealed as on the Roadster, while its rear window panel could be unzipped for better ventilation.

Ian and Pat Appleyard with their well known XK120 during the 1953 RAC Rally, the year after Ian won his Alpine Gold Cup. On this occasion they have a fine day for their run as they pass a small watching group.

The Jaguar stand at the 1953 New York Show with the centre piece the XK120 fixed-head coupé that set records at Montlhéry in August 1952 during its seven-day run. It is flanked by a Roadster and a Mk VII saloon.

Ian Appleyard at the wheel of his XK120 during the 1953 Morecambe Rally taking part in one of the special tests held on the sea front. A good crowd watches but all his concentration is on his task.

Taken at a 1952 show, this XK120 Roadster was finished off with gold-plated wire wheels and white-wall Dunlop tyres. A playboy touch and not really in the image of a record-breaking and race winning car.

A late model XK120 drop-head coupé and owner who have won a concours thanks to a fine turn out. The two-tone finish of the car is matched by the lady's outfit with the first set off by white-wall tyres on wire wheels.

Silverstone paddock in August 1956 with a C-type standing near a trio of 500cc cars. Not a major meeting, hence the casual air and lack of spectators, while the Jaguar carries a road tax disc so may well have been driven to the circuit.

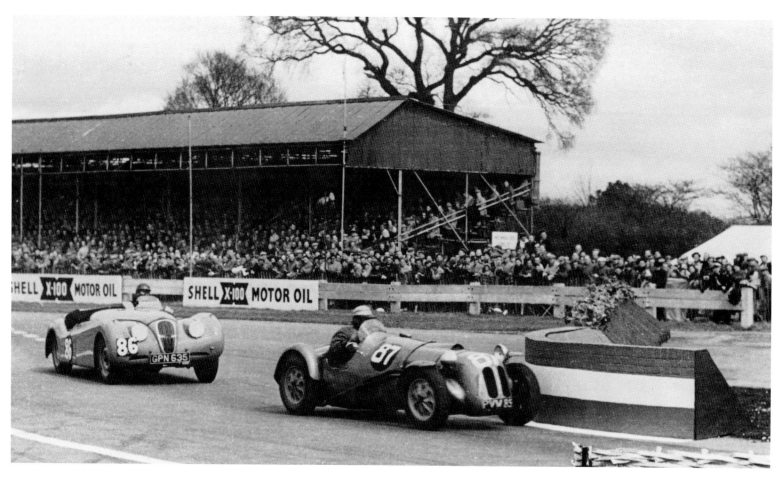

April 1953 and a BARC race meeting at Goodwood with a BMW just ahead of an XK120 Jaguar as they thread their way through the chicane. The BMW retired with no oil pressure but the left-hand drive Jaguar finished.

After the problems of 1952, it all came right for Jaguar at Le Mans in 1953 when Duncan Hamilton and Tony Rolt won with Stirling Moss and Peter Walker second in this C-type, and Peter Whitehead and Ian Stewart fourth in theirs.

The C-type XK120 in the form that succeeded at Le Mans in 1953 thanks to the changes that dealt with the overheating problems of the previous year. Smooth, sleek and capable, it was much helped by Dunlop disc brakes on all four wheels.

Third of the XK120 models was the drop-head coupé only built for 1953 and 1954. When folded, the top laid further back and under a cover compared to the Roadster where it went behind the seats and under the body tail out of sight. Still minimal body trim.

The C-type that won the 1953 Le Mans 24-hour race driven by Duncan Hamilton and Tony Rolt. They took the lead early in the event and stayed there despite the efforts of Ferrari, Alfa Romeo and Cunningham, the last to split the Jaguar team by taking third place behind Moss.

The Jaguar team for the 1953 Le Mans race with two cars carrying the Stirling Moss race number, the one on the left being the one that was used. Early on Moss stopped to change a plug and then to clear a choked fuel filter and it took many hours to climb back to second.

Jaguar sold 53 examples of the C-type and this one went to the USA, was licensed in Pennsylvania but is here at the Thompson Raceway in Connecticut where it no doubt gave a good account of itself.

This XK120C is at Bridgehampton, a small town on Long Island in New York state, and has a lock fitted to the petrol tank filler cap. Some of the space frame can be seen along with the AAA approval sticker.

A C-type fitted with the D-type cylinder head and three twin-choke Weber carburettors. With the bonnet hinged forward the front part of the space frame chassis can be seen along with other fittings that include a rear light mounted on the bulkhead to shine on the engine.

Driving seat of a C-type with its matching instruments that contra-rotate. For racing the rev-counter needle should be vertical at peak rpm to register at a glance and the speedometer needle should move in the same direction. Fly-off handbrake of course.

Le Mans in 1953 with one of the C-type cars at the pits with the bonnet up for checks and replenishment of oil, water or brake fluid while petrol goes into the tank at the other end. The filler caps will be sealed again before the car sets off.

When others disputed the Jaguar claim of world's fastest, the firm ran this XK120 at Jabbeke in Belgium in October, 1953. The headlights were cowled, an undershield fitted and the driver sat under a bubble top but the result was 172.41 mph over the two-way flying mile.

Soon to be replaced by a revised model, a 1954 XK120 Roadster still as clean, neat and tidy as when first launched late in 1948. Here with the optional wire wheels and with extra driving lights and a classic.

A fine line up of the C-type Jaguars run by Ecurie Ecosse of Scotland, a most successful team. Closest to the camera is a Connaught A-series car, an excellent Formula 2 vehicle of its day. The advertisements on the sides of the coaches used as transporters helped to defray running expenses.

Left: Jaguar took this car to Jabbeke in October, 1953, it having been prepared for Le Mans that year with much use of light alloys to reduce weight but not used, the C-types proving more than adequate. In Belgium it was timed at 178.38 mph.

Lined up on the start line at Goodwood in a C-type and awaiting the flag to fall. Always a time of tension whether a grand prix or a club meeting as a good start can make or mar a performance.

A left-hand drive XK120 drop-head coupé with the top down turning into the Rue du Boccador with a cheery wave. A fine picture that emphasises the clean-cut style of the model that made it such a success.

For 1954 racing Jaguar introduced the D-type that was based on a monocoque centre chassis constructed from sheet aluminium with a tubular front end to support the engine and suspension. Torsion bars front and rear supported the disc-braked wheels and a sleek body enclosed the works with a faired headrest behind the driver.

Taken during one of the wet periods of the 1954 Le Mans race with the D-type driven by Duncan Hamilton and Tony Rolt in the pits. They chased the leading Ferrari throughout the race but at the end had to settle for second place by just 2¹/2-miles, both cars covering over 2,500 miles in the day.

The drop-head coupé version of the XK120 only built for two years so less common than the others. The pressed-steel wheels were the standard fitment, always of 16-inch diameter, while the rear ones were concealed by spats locked at their top centre.

Working on the Hamilton/Rolt D-type that finished such a close second at the 1954 Le Mans 24-hour race under the watchful eye of Bill Lyons standing beside the car. A dry-sump lubrication system was used for the engine, hence the oil tank just behind the left front wheel, with its massive filler cap.

Driving room of a 1954 XK120 that changed little from 1948. The instruments had the rev-counter red band starting at 5,500 rpm and the petrol and ampere gauges switched over but the layout of the dials was not altered. Some switches moved, the ignition from top to bottom, and this owner added a reminder as to its position.

The three white bars across the nose of this C-type indicate that it is an Ecurie Ecosse entry. It is running at Goodwood in a 1954 BARC meeting and no doubt performed well.

Classic D-type with the head fairing, small wraparound screen for the driver, panel over the passenger area and spotlight faired in. Three ears on the hub nuts to ensure that one was always in place for a clout and pressed-steel wheels with disc brakes behind them.

Intake side of the six-cylinder, twin-cam 3½-litre Jaguar engine with its three twin-choke Weber carburettors that could take the D-type to over 170 mph. A fabricated sub-frame supported it from the front bulkhead with radiator and header tank at the front and the HT leads curling over the cam box to the plugs.

This Mk VII was close by the Arc de Triomphe in Paris during a stage of the 1954 Monte Carlo Rally. A big car for such an event, but a comfortable one well able to cope with most of the terrain encountered on the way south and keep its occupants warm and dry during their long journey.

Rear three-quarter view of the D-type showing its fine lines that were to take it to three Le Mans victories. Trailing arms located the live rear axle with torsion bars to provide the springing.

This XK120 was competing in an event held on the Silverstone Club circuit in 1961. A cowl has been added at the front to encourage air to flow through the radiator and removal of the front bumper assisted this.

Start of a race, for Mk VII Jaguar and Daimler Century cars, held during the 1954 Daily Express Trophy meeting at Silverstone long before Jaguar took Daimler over. Note how Stirling Moss, on the left, has already gained a second or two on the field, as usual, for he raced from the fall of the flag and a second here could be easier to find than on the circuit.

Cockpit and engine of the D-type with few instruments and no gear lever knob at this point. Starter button on the left and only the necessary switches for ignition and lights. One of the disc brakes and the front suspension wishbone can also be seen.

The classic D-type shape with the bonnet buckled down and all ready to go places fast. Note how the wheel balance weights were bolted in place between the lightning holes and not clipped to the rim where they could come adrift.

Few D-types can have been as well polished as this one. On the wall a poster urges all to visit the Montagu Motor Museum at Beaulieu and carries a BP sponsor logo, this being where they housed the prototype that finished second at Le Mans in 1954.

Rear view of the 1954 D-type as seen by most drivers at Le Mans that year when it finished so close to the Ferrari that won. Revenge came over the next three years.

The exhaust side of the 3.4-litre, twin-cam engine of the D-type showing the pipes in branches of three, twin breathers from the cam box, the oil tank and part of the chassis.

Somewhere in the USA an XK120 Roadster finds itself surrounded by Detroit sedans. The year is 1955 so tail fins have begun to appear but would grow more extreme in the next few years. Fashions would change too while fast-food outlets had yet to come.

Intake side of the D-type with the bonnet up to expose some of the construction methods used for this substantial item that had to open and close quickly, easily and positively every time. No battery fitted here but accessible for a quick change if needed.

Front three-quarter view of the D-type from where the twin exhaust pipes can be seen emerging just in front of the rear wheel. On the C-type the spot light had fitted behind the grill but the side location out of the air stream to the radiator was better.

Left: Rivers Fletcher went motor racing and is seen here with his two sons and Dennis Ibbotson with the HWM Jaguar at his home. Six exhausts on the left side and a neat single-seat racing car. A year or two later a two-seat HWM Jaguar was built for sports car racing.

An artists drawing of a car that never was. It shows the fixed-head coupé XK120 but with the front grill of the XK140 that replaced it and had a longer passenger compartment.

The big saloon became the Mk VIIM for 1955 with more power, Borg-Warner automatic transmission, horn grills below the headlights and wraparound rear bumpers. This one was once owned by the Queen Mother and later converted to a Mk IX specification with disc brakes and other improvements.

In 1954 the XK140 replaced the older model with rack-and-pinion steering underneath and heavier bumpers and trim on the outside. There was more power with the C-type cylinder head an option if a further increase was desired while the engine was mounted further forward. This is the drop-head coupé version.

The XK140 Roadster followed the existing lines but offered more compartment space with the engine moved forward. At the rear the boot lid stopped short above the bumper line while the car remained a two-seater. The monument stands in gardens in Leamington in honour of Edward Willes of Newbold Comyn who donated their site.

The fixed-head coupé version of the XK140 had the roof line raised and run further back so that rear seats could be added, albeit very cramped. It did give more luggage space but the change to the line was not to all tastes. Much heavier front bumper.

Also an occasional four-seater, the drop-head coupé XK140 continued with the rear window panel that could be zipped out for added ventilation. The front end style was noticeably heavier than before but the original line remained.

Interior of the XK140 coupé with sliding door handles high up out of the way but little was altered on the facia. A radio replaced the standard small drawer at centre and this example had a watch and stop watch added for rally use where timing accuracy was vital. The fly-off hand-brake was dropped for the early XK140 but returned for 1957.

For 1955 Jaguar introduced the 2.4-litre compact saloon fitted with a 2483cc version of the existing engine having a shorter stroke. This went into a monocoque body shell sitting on coil springs at the front, and the result offered all the Jaguar style and fitments without the bulk of the Mk VII. This one is on the Jaguar stand at the London Motor Show at Earls Court.

The XK140 proved just as popular for club competition events as its predecessor and this 1955 fixed-head coupé is turning down Paddock Bend at the Brands Hatch circuit in Kent during a 1956 race. A demanding corner then and now.

Frontal aspect of a 1955 XK140 fixed-head coupé showing the larger bumper with overiders, turn signals in the lower wings, heavier grill and wipers that worked in opposition to each other. The leaping cat mascot on the bonnet has been added for it was not an option until the XK150 arrived.

The interior of an XK140 coupé that has been modified for rallies, hence the extra switches and dials to the right of the steering wheel, in front of the passenger and on the centre console. Automatic transmission on this car from Borg-Warner so a late model with the fly-off hand brake.

Fine Mk VIIM, with an XK140 right behind it, at a 1956 rally. The owner has fitted the leaping cat mascot to the bonnet; years later such items were banned for pedestrian safety reasons so could no longer be used on the street.

An XK140 drop-head coupé on show and gleaming under the lights. The whitewall tyres set off the black finish well as do the wire wheels on knock-off hubs that they are fitted to. Left-hand drive and a marginal four-seater for short rides, a great two-seater for the long ones.

Side view of the new 1955 2.4-litre seen at the London Motor Show held at Earls Court late in the year. The whitewall tyres set off the black body colour and the graceful lines of a very successful car.

This 1955 XK140 drop-head coupé was taking part in a rally held the next year when pictured. The badges on their mounting bar indicate the owner's interests and enthusiasm, and include several of the best known national clubs.

A fine sunny day so the front and rear quarter windows are both open on this 1955 XK140 fixed-head coupé. An occasion when the drop-head or the Roadster might be preferred but in Britain rain is seldom far away.

Taken at the 1955 Paris Show, this Jaguar, said to be an XK140, had a body by Ghia, one of the best Italian coachbuilding firms, but proving once again that the styles of the two countries did not mix well. Gone is the Jaguar line but there in none of the Italian flair in its place.

Left: Down by the river for a photo session for this lady and the XK140 drop-head coupé with its top up. A fine setting for the car to show off its line and style that suggest performance in the best manner.

Only 73 XK140 Roadster cars were built with right-hand drive so this was a rare model. This one is seen taking part in a 6-hour relay race organised by the 750 Motor Club at Silverstone in August 1954. Good fun for all those involved.

H.M. The Queen with William Lyons and the D-type Jaguar that won the tragic 1955 Le Mans 24-hour race driven by Mike Hawthorn and Ivor Bueb. The visit to the factory took place in 1956 when Jaguar would win Le Mans again, repeating this in 1957 as well.

Pinin Farina produced this four-seater coupé in 1956 using the Mk VII saloon as the basis. The separate chassis made it easy to create a totally new body style but, once again, the result lacked Italian flair and lost the original British Jaguar line while something of the USA crept in.

Said to be a 1956 XK140 fitted with a body built by Boano and designed by Raymond Loewy, the result was certainly dramatic but quite unacceptable for a British Jaguar. Loewy produced many fine designs but this was not one of them.

This was Jaguar, the 1956 D-type at Le Mans that year driven by J. Swaters and M. Rousselle, a Belgian entry that finished fourth behind the three works cars led home by Ron Flockhart and Ivor Bueb. The first two cars were entered by Ecurie Ecosse, the third by a French entrant.

Three-quarter view of the Raymond Loewy body design constructed by Boano of Turin on a Jaguar XK140 chassis. Possibly intended for the North American market, it failed to make any impact so no more was heard of it.

The Mk VIII came along for 1956 and is seen here late in the previous year at the Earls Court London Motor Show. Compared to the older model, the grill was altered, a one-piece curved windscreen replaced the split type, and a two-tone finish was offered for this large, fast car.

Side view of a 1956 Mk VII fitted with a two-door coupé body by Pinin Farina. Although it retains some of its British style, the Italian changes do neither country justice and lack of enthusiasm is highlighted by the soft front tyre.

Side view of a 1957 Mk VIII with the two-tone finish and complete with leaping cat mascot on the bonnet. The addition of the chrome trim strip on the side plus a rear wheel spat that exposed more wheel gave the car a lighter line although it remained heavy but fast.

Enthusiasts soon found that the 2.4-litre compact saloon made an excellent competition car. This 1956 model is heavily engaged with an XK120 during a 1961 race at Silverstone and had the drum brakes and narrow rear track of the early cars built up to 1959.

One of the works D-type cars at Le Mans in 1956. Driven by Mike Hawthorn and Ivor Bueb it finished sixth but Ninian Sanderson and Ron Flockhart won in a car entered by Ecurie Ecosse. Just one entry and they won, in 1957 they had two entries and were first and second.

Detail of the left front corner of some D-type cars had both the headlight and a spotlight mounted under clear perspex covers to assist the airflow.

Mike Hawthorn in the D-type he shared with Ivor Bueb in the 1956 Le Mans 24-hour race in which they finished sixth after losing some 90 minutes early in the event with engine problems.

Ian Appleyard taking part in one of the final tests of the 1956 RAC Rally that were held at Blackpool and in which he was runner up in his XK140 coupé. Rather different from the SS100 built for him in 1946 but the skill remained the same.

The Ecurie Ecosse team of D-type cars line up at Monza in 1957 for the Monza 500 race held in three heats. They were run on the high speed banked circuit with ten Indianapolis cars also taking part and lap speeds were in excess of 163 mph. The Jaguars finished fourth, fifth and sixth to greatly impress the US visitors.

Further view of the 1956 Mk VII with two-door four-seat body by Pinin Farina with its American style for the front that fails to sit well with the Italianised British form of the main body line.

The 2.4-litre compact saloon was joined by a 3.4-litre model in 1957 and this offered more performance than the stiffened monocoque body shell could really handle. A top speed close to 120 mph was fine, but it still had the drum brakes with the rear spats amended to improve cooling air flow, although discs were a 1958 option.

Lining up for the start of the 1958 four-hour Tourist Trophy race run at Goodwood in September. Bill Lyons listens to a driver, possibly Moss who led a trio of Aston Martin cars to the first three places while Masten Gregory and Innes Ireland took D-type Jaguar number 4 to fifth place. Not their day.

Le Mans in 1957 for the 24-hour race won by this Jaguar driven by Ron Flockhart and Ivor Bueb. Ninian Sanderson and J. Lawrence were second in the other Ecurie Ecosse D-type, both with 3.8-litre engines, followed home by French and Belgian 3.4-litre D-types.

In 1957 the XK150 appeared in Roadster and drop-head coupé forms as well as this fixed-head coupé. Wider and with a much higher wing line it continued to be a part-time four-seater, better suited for two with luggage. Disc brakes all round offered great improvement in that area and most cars had the optional wire wheels and knock-off hubs.

Roadster version of the XK150 introduced in 1958 with one-piece windscreen and wind-up windows in place of the side screens of the past. The pressed-steel wheels were the standard build, but seldom fitted, although where they were they came with the rear wheel spats as always.

The D-type, like the C-type before it, was built for general sale with a shorter nose more suited to club and national competition use. However, sales were slow so 16 cars were converted to this XK-SS form with full road equipment while retaining the D-type engine and brakes.

The 3.4-litre compact saloon that had more performance than chassis or brakes if pushed too hard. When it and its smaller version were revised to Mk II form, the originals became referred to as the Mk I although never designated as such by the factory.

The XK150 series began with the 3441cc version of the well established twin-cam engine with first one and then two more powerful types becoming available. From 1959 the 3781cc engine became an alternative.

Clean 3.4-litre Mk I saloon taking a special test during a 1958 rally, most likely on the private roads of a service establishment. The hub caps have gone missing from this car, perhaps to ready it for a wheel changing test.

An XK140 fixed-head coupé taking part in a 1957 hill climb, the type of event the owner could enjoy without exceeding a personal limit or coming into contact with another car through his or their mistake. If you hit the scenery then it was your fault alone.

Final form of the XK series was the 150 with its high waistline and built in all three body forms. The fixed-head coupé was perhaps the best for the British weather, the others more suited to sunny climates.

Front end of the XK150 Roadster with its one-piece windscreen and a wider bonnet that made working on the engine an easier task. The grill reverted more to the lighter form of the XK120 and the front bumper was restyled in the centre to lose some of the heavy look of the XK140. The twin wipers now moved in tandem as one.

This XK-SS has the hood down but betrays its D-type origins. Because they are rare they are valuable and further confusion with them arose when some where altered back to D-type while some D-types were changed into XK-SS models for road use.

Arch enthusiast, special builder, writer and commentator John Bolster with a 1959 XK150 fixed-head coupé. With his years of experience John would have extracted full performance from this car and enjoyed it to the full.

The early 3.4-litre compact saloon, later known as the Mk I, kept to the existing engine and was available with manual, overdrive and automatic transmissions. This is a 1958 model so may have the optional disc brakes while the brief rear spats confirm that it is the larger of the two models.

Many 3.4-litre saloons went racing despite the limitations of the narrow rear track. This one is at Silverstone in 1961 but the car dates from 1958 and has had the rear spats removed for its race.

A 1958 XK150 fixed-head coupé parked in a pleasant setting to have its picture taken. The wire wheels on their knock-off hubs were an option and required the removal of the rear spats while the white-wall tyres were a further option.

The Mk IX replaced the older saloon in 1958 with the adoption of the 3781cc engine and disc brakes for all four wheels. The line was as for the Mk VIII but power steering was standard and most had automatic transmission. All remained thirsty with a 220 bhp engine to feed, but were fast and comfortable.

Duncan Hamilton at the wheel of his D-type negotiating the Goodwood chicane during the Tourist Trophy held in September 1958. A successful driver over a decade, he had shared the winning Jaguar at Le Mans in 1953 and been second the following year. At Goodwood the Aston Martin team dominated and number six had to settle for sixth place.

Most XK150 models had the wire wheels and knock-off hubs as does this Roadster so went without the rear spats. Later cars had the option of the 3781cc engine and both this and the 3.4-litre were available in different states of tune.

The famous Jaguar leaping cat bonnet mascot here attached to a 2.4-litre compact saloon. It appeared on most models at one time or another, often as an added option along with the chrome bonnet strips in front and behind it, until the safety lobby banned it.

Rear view of a 1959 XK150 Roadster as seen by most other drivers. The round boot badge listed the five Le Mans victories as well as giving the model code, while the number plate lamp had the marque name moulded into the rear facing area.

Three-quarter front view of a 1959 Mk IX saloon that carries the leaping cat mascot on its bonnet. A big car and the last to have a separate chassis frame so the final development of a series that could be traced back to prewar days. As always, it offered a great deal of well appointed car for the money.

The XK150 Roadster in 1958 with the top raised and clearly showing the line that traced back to the first XK120. William Lyons would produce the style by instructing skilled sheet-metal workers to construct a prototype under his direction and once he was satisfied the result would be turned into production drawings.

Time has past and the demand for a D-type resulted in replicas being built. This one carries a price tag of £9,500, a fraction of the price a genuine car with good provenance would fetch.

This time an XK150 fixed-head coupé leaning over as it negotiates a corner at Silverstone during a 200-mile relay race held in 1959. A lady driver in this case, just as quick as anyone else despite the errant wiper blade lifting into the eye sight line.

The Mk IX saloon that used the 3.8-litre engine to push it along at speeds up to 115 mph and well able to cruise at 80 to 90 mph until more fuel was needed for its 17-gallon tank after around 200 miles although Jaguar suggested 300. But unlikely unless kept down to 60 mph.

A gaggle of Mk II saloons leaving the start line at a Goodwood race meeting. They were popular and successful at many events, had little trouble seeing off the Riley and Sunbeam in row three, but needed to beware the Mini that would lead them all in time.

Before the days of cassette tape players and long before the CD player, Philips developed a record player for the car. It took the then popular 7-inch records one at a time so a passenger was an essential to feed them in. The car is an XK150 in which the hand brake was fitted on the driver's side of the centre console.

March 1961 and the Geneva Motor Show saw Jaguar introduce the replacement for the XK series, the fabulous E-type that combined the best of the past with the future. Under the long bonnet went the fully proven 3.8-litre, twin-cam engine with its three carburettors and 265 bhp. Over the mechanics went a monocoque body shell with breath-taking lines, initially in fixed-head coupé form.

The E-type coupé was soon joined by an open Roadster for which an optional hard top was available. The gearbox remained the old Jaguar four-speed unit with no synchromesh for first, but there was independent suspension all round as well as the disc brakes. Here, Bill Lyons is about to take a drive.

Open E-type that copied the D-type in that the monocoque shell had a square-tube sub-frame attached to the bulkhead to carry the engine and front suspension. The bonnet hinged forward to give good access to the engine and early cars had an external latch on each side to hold it down, these later moved inside the car.

Loading a very early E-type for a flight out to a show, hence the photographers on the steps. This car has the external bonnet latch with chrome cover used at first and is the open Roadster with the top up and then protected. A tight squeeze in the aircraft and awkward to load and unload without damage.

Early E-type Roadsters had three windscreen wipers so would not be worried by the rain falling on cars, people and the factory offices. Over 50 cars ready for delivery in 1961 and early ones so this could be the first batch of a series than ran to over 75,000 cars during a decade or more.

An E-type attending a rally in 1961 that required the headlights to be taped over. Quick-action jack to lift both wheel up at once with hub nut and mallet close to hand. In later years the nut would lose its ears due to safety legislation.

Same E-type with its top raised while taking part in a competitive event. At a rather higher level of competition, two coupés ran at Le Mans in 1962 as private entries to finish fourth and fifth behind three Ferraris.

Early fixed-head coupé E-type that was a true Gran Turismo car able to cruise with ease at 100 mph carrying two and their luggage. The rear hatch hinged to the side and gave access to a good sized storage area for the cases while the price remained highly competitive.

Roadster E-type with the 3.8-litre engine, triple wiper blades and the pure clean line that took it to over 140 mph. The early seats looked fine but were later replaced by a more comfortable form while the dynamo electrics were hardly up to the performance of the car.

Loading a Mk X at Southampton for shipment to the USA. The model replaced the older saloon in 1961 and introduced a monocoque body structure with all-round independent suspension along with the disc brakes. A limited-slip differential took the power from the 3.8-litre engine with its three carburettors and most cars had automatic transmission.

Four headlights appeared on the Mk X and would remain for many future models while the car was big and wider than most with bulging sides and thick doors. It could still accommodate five with ease but remained heavy and thirsty, retained too much of the Mk IX line, and was seen as old-fashioned in many markets.

The Mk II versions of the compact saloons had a wider rear track, disc brakes, larger rear window and thinner window pillars. The larger model was also available with the 3781cc engine and the 3.8 Mk II proved both fast on the road and very competitive on race circuits.

A small number of lightweight E-types were built for racing and these had an aluminium body, a special engine with aluminium block and the suspension suitably modified. The body was formed as a Roadster with the hardtop added.

Front end of a 1962 Mk X saloon with its four lights, twin horns, wraparound bumpers and small leaping cat mascot. The style with the whole front leaning forward, as if to pounce, continued in use for many years, only becoming more rounded in the 1990s.

Rear quarter view of a lightweight E-type with the hardtop added to the aluminium Roadster body. Built in the early-1960s by the factory competition department, some cars later had other bodies fitted by their owners to meet a specific need. They were good but sports car racing moved on faster.

In 1963 Jaguar took this Mk II saloon to Monza to run on the banked circuit and ran it round for close to four days to cover 10,000 miles at an average speed of 106.58 mph. In the process they collected four class C International records and the car is seen here on the last day.

From 1963 the Mk II Jaguar was available as this 2¹/2-litre V8 Daimler fitted with the 2548cc V-8 overhead-valve engine designed by Edward Turner of Triumph motorcycle fame. It was mated to a Borg-Warner automatic transmission in nearly all cases, had a revised interior with bench front seat, and the traditional Daimler radiator flutes.

The Turner-designed Daimler V-8 engine was first used for the SP250 sports two-seater seen here being assembled with glass-fibre body, disc brakes and 120 mph potential. Built up to 1964 with the engine to continue in the Jaguar Mk II shell to 1969.

Monza 1963 and the Mk II about to start its 10,000 mile run, often in poor weather conditions with rain and fog. It cruised at 114 mph, consumed fuel at just over 14 mpg, which meant over 700 gallons, and sported a second windscreen wiper blade on the roof line.

Fine Mk X seen in 1964, the year the engine capacity was increased to 4228cc by enlarging the bore. Synchromesh for all four gears in rare manual form and improved power steering system but still large, long, heavy and thirsty. In this form a good car with an old line.

Rear quarter of a 1964 E-type Roadster fitted with the 3.8-litre engine, this the last year of that capacity and still with no synchromesh on first gear. From any angle a great shape although luggage space was restricted in the boot but added to by using the space behind the seats.

Rear seat interior of a 1964 Mk X saloon that began to use the 4.2-litre engine that year. Walnut trim on the back of the front seats, ashtrays and fold-down occasional tables followed that of the front seat area, lots of footroom under the seats and all very traditional in the British style.

Series I, as it became known once the II appeared, E-type of 1964, the year of change to the 4.2-litre engine and gearbox with synchromesh on all four speeds. There was also an alternator to improve the electrics and better seats among the many changes.

Interior of the E-type had the main instruments in front of the driver and the minor ones in the centre. The confusing line of identical switches was not unusual at the time, before most moved to become mounted close to the steering wheel for finger-tip control.

For 1964 Jaguar introduced the S-type that combined the front end of the Mk II, with some changes to the grill and wings, with the Mk X rear to provide independent rear suspension. Powered by the 3.4- or 3.8-litre engine it was longer than the Mk II so had more rear legroom and luggage space without the Mk X bulk.

Having taken the Mk II and given it a Mk X rear to create the S-type, Jaguar then changed the front to the Mk X format to arrive at this 420. In effect a slimmer and lighter Mk X, it used the 4.2-litre engine and was also badged as the Daimler Sovereign.

This D-type was fitted with a two-door coupé body by Michelotti and exhibited at the 1963 Geneva show and proved a successful combination of British chassis design and Italian coachbuilding style. The wheels with the three-eared hub nuts were pure D-type while the body showed how good Italian lines could be.

Hoisting an E-type aboard for its shipment to an export market. The USA took many of these but it was just as desirable to customers in many other countries all over the world. The line is as perfect from this angle as from any other.

In 1966 the 420G replaced the Mk X saloon with some minor changes but its appearance brought about some confusion as the 420 model was introduced at the same time, being smaller and with its origins from the Mk II and S-type cars. The 420G continued as the big Jaguar saloon until 1970, with some two dozen built as limousines.

The Jaguar E-type assembly line at the Browns Lane, Coventry, factory with Roadster and Coupé models nearing completion. Without bonnets fitted, the line of the twin-cam engine and its triple SU carburettors was clear and the year was 1967 so the cars are Series I with the 4.2-litre engine.

Bertone was another Italian styling house to use the Jaguar as a base for its own line. This two-door, fixed-head coupé had a 3.8-litre engine and some details that followed those of the Jaguar saloons.

JAGUAR 3,8 FT BODY BY BERTONE

bertone

By 1966 the E-type was powered by the 4.2-litre engine and available in 2+2 coupé form with the body extended and the roofline raised. The added space was more useful for extra luggage than people, much as for the XK-series, but the existing coupé remained available.

Under the bonnet of a 420 or Daimler Sovereign saloon showing the well developed twin-cam engine, its three SU carburettors and remote radiator header tank. Although the engine was coming up to its 20th birthday, it still performed well in all versions and models.

The interior of the 2+2 E-type in 1966 with the same dials and switches with markings that were hard to decipher in daylight and had to be found be feel at night. Improved seats, a glove box and a change of trim, while the extra length of this model enabled the Borg-Warner automatic transmission to be an option, the only E-type six to have this listed.

In the mid-1960s Jaguar built this one-off XJ13 prototype for possible use at Le Mans in the 24-hour race. It was powered by a V-12 engine installed just behind the driver while the body line was not too far removed from that of the E-type.

From this angle the open top and perspex engine cover of the XJ13 are clearly seen. The body line was of the period although most Le Mans cars were soon coupés due to their high speeds, an easy change to make.

Right: The XJ13 engine in show condition but without the intakes or injection pipes. Its capacity was 4993cc and it produced 502 bhp at 7,600 rpm with the camshafts driven from the crankshaft nose and the aluminium sump having front and rear wells for the oil.

Left: The engine of the XJ13 was a 60-degree V-12 with twin-overhead camshafts for each bank and fuel injection into the fine array of bell-mouth intakes. It sat under a perspex cover so the details were clear to all when the car was shown but a metal one would have been fitted if the car had ever raced.

The Daimler limousine line continued from 1968 with the DS420 that used the Jaguar 420G floorpan and the 4.2-litre twin-cam engine so had independent suspension all round. While few Jaguar limousines were built, and then only to 1970, the Daimler ran on to 1992. This one is in Knightsbridge, just off Sloane Street in London.

The Series II E-type arrived for 1968 in all three body styles, this the 2+2. The headlights were no longer cowled in and the windscreen was raked so its lower edge was further forward. Safety legislation removed the hub nut ears so a special spanner was added to the tool kit to fit the hexagon nut and still offer three ears to the clouting mallet.

For 1968 the Mk II became the 240 and this 340 with the existing body shell but a reduced specification to avoid competing with the new XJ6 saloon. The larger capacity was only built for one season, the smaller for two and then they were gone but the Mk II left good memories for many.

This Bertone two-door coupé was based on an E-type and known as the Jaguar Piranha. A 1967 design, it had something of the Corvette in its line but somehow lacked a real British, Italian or American style, although was no doubt well made and appointed.

Introduced late in 1968, the XJ6 was acclaimed Car of the Year in 1969 and took over from the 420G, the 420 and the Mk II models. Offered with the 2.8- and 4.2-litre, six-cylinder engines, it was a brilliant design in the Jaguar tradition that would run for many years in various formats despite some quality control problems of the 1970s when Jaguar were part of British Leyland.

The Series II E-type Roadster of 1969 with the grill bar now part of the bumper, exposed headlights moved further forward, revised positions for the turn and parking lights, and hexagon nuts for the wire wheels. The 4.2-litre engine had a restricted output for the US models but a change of axle ratio kept the acceleration up to the mark.

Taken in 1967 at the Expo held that year in Montreal, this was a late Series I Roadster with some of the interim changes such as the exposed headlights, but it retained the small intake opening at the front, separate bumpers, triple wipers and original minor light locations. Must be the British section and a Mini follows the Jaguar.

Dockside picture of the 240 saloon only offered for two seasons and a low-cost version of the older Mk II. It brought the compact saloon line to its close after more than a decade, leaving many owners with fond memories.

The E-type, especially in restricted USA form, needed more capacity to regain its ability for relaxed, high-speed cruising and this arrived in 1971 with the Series III. This was powered by a 5344cc, V-12, overhead-camshaft engine and both Roadster and Coupé models went on the longer 2+2 wheelbase so automatic transmission was available to either.

Engine bay of the Series III E-type showing the four carburettors that fed it, the front air intakes that fed them, and some of the front-end chassis frame work that supported the engine and carried the front suspension as well as the bonnet. A fine array of pipes, cables, connectors and linkages while an early form of electronic ignition was employed.

The XJ6 established a new line for the Jaguar saloon by combining elements from several models of the past. It kept the existing twin-cam six engine but this gave it ample performance while manual or automatic transmissions catered for the preferences of home market and export customers.

The luggage space offered by the XJ6 saloon line, here with the 4.2-litre engine installed, enabled it to cater for most needs, being long enough for a set of golf clubs, even if a trifle shallow. From all angles the car had style allied to its performance.

Above: The 4.2-litre version of the XJ6 saloon in a picturesque setting to have its photo taken. The line is clearly descended from the 420G with a touch of the flared wheel arches of the E-type. Slim window frames and plenty of glass area resulted in a light and spacious passenger compartment.

Below right: The new saloon was upgraded to become the XJ12 in 1972 with the 5344cc V-12 engine as had been intended from the start. A tight squeeze under the bonnet, it pushed the car along to 150 mph in silence, although with a considerable appetite for petrol. A different grill and special badge indicated the model that was only built on the original XJ6 wheelbase for one season, otherwise on the longer type.

Red Square in Moscow in 1972 with a Series III E-type coupé being studied by one and all. Few, if any, other cars of this type can have stood on the same spot at that time for officials travelled in large saloons and the populace in what they could muster.

Late in 1972 the XJ12L joined the range with more room in the back and a year later took Series II form with numerous changes to suit North American safety standards. Among these was a wider and shallower grill, raised front bumper and drop-down over-riders to protect the enlarged air intake below it.

The XJ series had its counterpart in the Daimler range produced by badge engineering and minor trim changes. The XJ6 became the Sovereign and the XJ12 the Double-Six. This 1974 Series II version has the alternative two-door coupé body to come later for Jaguar. At back is a 1931 Double Six sports model that had a 7-foot bonnet on a par with that of the first SS1.

Engine assembly at the Browns Lane, Coventry, factory with a 5.3-litre V-12 nearing completion. Behind is another at a much earlier stage while in the background sits a pile of components. Special tools and fixtures plus air-driven spanners speeded up the process for the operator.

The Series III E-type Roadster with the 5.3-litre V-12 engine was built up to 1974 and proved a most successful and desirable road car. They were raced but the longer wheelbase made them less suited for this than the early cars, and by the start of the 1970s competition sports cars had advanced a good deal from 1961.

Interior of the 1966 E-type 2+2 coupé with the longer wheelbase but limited rear legroom. Intended more for couples with children it had adequate luggage space under the side-hinged boot lid. The spare wheel went under the boot floor so a puncture would mean removing all luggage to get it out.

A Series III E-type prepared for racing by Huffaker Engineering and driven to the model's first USA victory at Seattle by Lee Mueller in August 1974. Still with bumpers front and rear but a very shallow screen and a roll bar to protect the driver.

Fine study of the E-type Roadster fitted with the glass-fibre hardtop in its Series III form with the big V-12 engine. Pressed-steel wheels although the wire ones remained an option and only two seats. The small over-riders had rubber inserts, much enlarged for 1974 cars destined for the USA.

In 1975 British Leyland planned to race a pair of XJ12C coupés in the European Touring Car Championship and arranged for Broadspeed Engineering to prepare them rather than the highly experienced Jaguar race shop. They were run as Leyland Cars and the first was shown at Silverstone in March 1976 but it was the end of the season before one ran in anger. It qualified on pole but retired in the race.

Interesting exercise by Pininfarina shown at Geneva in 1979. Based on the XJ series it resulted in a Spider two-door body with extremely sleek lines, concealed headlights and a real Italian line but no indication as to which engine went under the hood.

The Daimler Sovereign took on a Series II form for 1974, as did the XJ6, and was listed in the long wheelbase saloon form as here and a shorter two-door coupé from 1975. Both 3.4- and 4.2-litre engines were offered and most saloons had automatic transmission.

Engine room of the British Leyland XJ12C coupé prepared by Broadspeed Engineering who were never given enough time to get the car both fast and reliable. The result was one outing in 1976 and many in 1977 where the two cars were always fast but seldom finished, usually retiring when leading. Popular with racing fans but not BL who then retired from the fray.

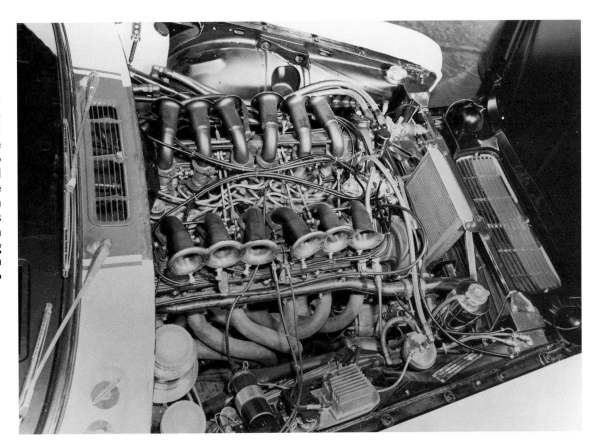

The Series II Daimler Sovereign in its two-door coupé form and fitted with the 4.2-litre engine. First seen as an XJ6C Jaguar late in 1973, it was 1975 before either reached the market due to some door and window sealing problems. Built on the shorter wheelbase with fine lines.

Jaguar did not produce estate cars so this was one that had been modified by Avon to that type. It was based on a 1983 Daimler Double-Six Series III car and was itself a Mk 2 version whose lines fitted in well with the base model. The flutes on the housing for the number plate were retained as usual for any Daimler.

By the time the XJ12C reached production in 1975, along with the XJ6C, it had been re-coded as the XJ5.3C. Both models were very elegant and the larger was good for close to 150 mph but consumed fuel at an equally high speed. The hike in petrol price and the poor race results from the Leyland exercise damaged sales so production was limited and sadly stopped in 1977.

In place of the coupé version of the XJ series came the XJ-S in a two-door style of its own that would run on to 1992. It had a shorter wheelbase, the 5.3-litre V-12 engine, four seats with limited rear room and great speed. Stylish, fast and successful.

The XJ-S drank petrol so it was inevitable that a smaller version would be built which led to the XJ-S3.6 in coupé and this cabriolet form with Targa-type roof panels that lifted out. It was powered by a 3590cc twin-cam, six-cylinder engine with 24 valves from the new AJ6 series that finally began to replace the old and faithful XK unit.

Martin Brundle in the XJR-9 prepared by TWR for top level sports car races in the 1980s. The team won the 24-hour event at Le Mans and Daytona in 1988 and 1990, and took the world title in 1987 and 1988 under Tom Walkinshaw's able leadership. By 1990 they were running the cars in XJR-12 form.

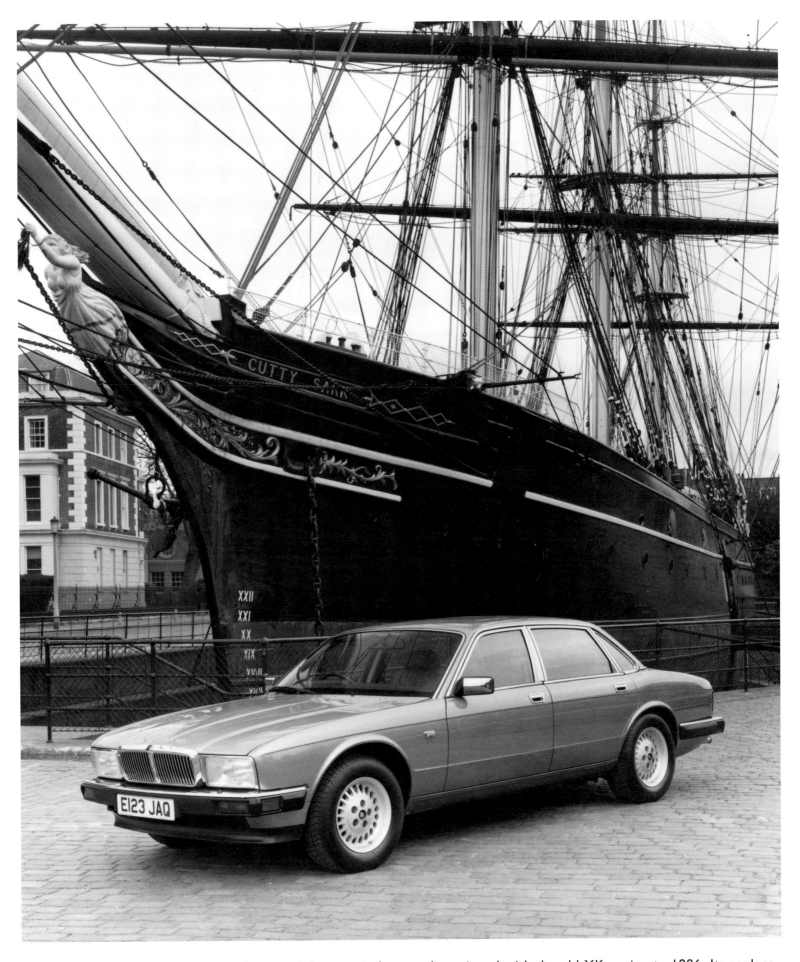

The original XJ6 reached Series III form with larger windows and continued with the old XK engine to 1986. Its replacement was coded as the XJ40 while in development and fitted the new 3590cc 24-valve, six-cylinder engine. The base model and the Vanden Plas sold in the USA had four round headlights but the Sovereign model, that shared the Daimler name, fitted these larger single light units on each side.

From the start the two-door coupé had the interesting style where the rear quarter panels rose up on each side of the low-set boot lid. At first it fitted the V-12 engine and then the new, 24-valve six as in this XJ-S3.6 of 1988, five years into the model run. A suitable location with the firm winning at Le Mans that year.

The Jaguar Sport XJR3.6 model listed from 1988 was based on the standard model but had revised suspension, a deeper front spoiler and some trim changes. The engine was stock and drove automatic transmission, but for 1990 a 3980cc unit in uprated form was used with a choice of drive systems.

This view shows the rear quarter panels that were a feature of all the XJ-S coupés. The HE version was first seen in 1982, the letters standing for High Efficiency and the fitment of new cylinder heads that resulted in more power from the V-12 engine. The wheels were new but the rear passenger space remained minimal while fuel consumption could be prodigious.

The Jaguar Sport theme was extended to produce this XJR-S coupé for 1989 with a rear spoiler and Speedline wheels. Late in the year the 5.3-litre V-12 engine was opened up to 5985cc and the power raised further for 1991. Behind stands one of the XJR sports racing cars that had many successes.

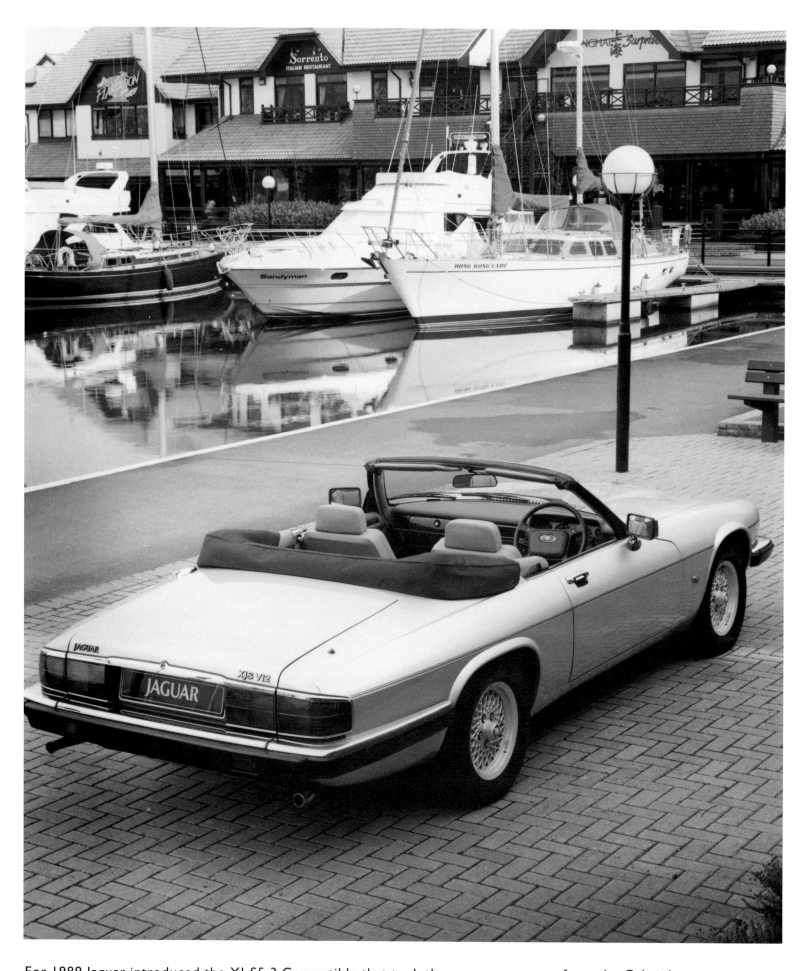

For 1989 Jaguar introduced the XJ-S5.3 Convertible that took the open concept on from the Cabriolet to a true open body. It kept the existing engine and transmission but had the body structure stiffened and a power-operated top, the rear windows rising and falling with this. A two-seater model with space for luggage behind the seats, it was a very desirable version of the XJ-S series.

By 1991 the firm was running the XJR-14 in sports car races and took the team title by a good margin. Derek Warwick drives this one and finished runner-up in the driver championship to Teo Fabi who won, also driving a Jaguar, the team winning three of the eight events that counted with several other good places.

The XJ220 was first seen at the 1988 British Motor Show as a concept performance car to match any other in the world. Then it had the V-12 engine and four-wheel drive but when it reached production in 1991, built by a joint Jaguar/TWR set up in its own small factory, it had a 3498cc V-6 alloy engine with twin-overhead camshafts. This was fitted with twin turbochargers and 24 valves, was installed behind the seats and drove a five-speed gearbox. Very expensive.

Jaguar took their new supercar racing in XJ220-C form and at Le Mans in 1993 the one surviving car, of three, finished 15th and won the GT class, quite a performance in an arduous event. The drivers were John Nielsen, David Brabham and David Coulthard while one car had previously run well at a Silverstone meeting.

The XJ-S simply ran on and on, either with the V-12 engine as in this example, or with the 3.6-litre six. This car has the four headlights always used for cars exported to the USA, those sold in Europe having a single, lozenge-shaped unit on each side. Some US owners would have these fitted to their cars to acquire the original style.

From late in 1994 the saloon was listed in XJR form powered at first by a 4.0-litre supercharged six-cylinder engine but later joined by this version with an all-alloy supercharged, quad-cam V-8 of the same size. The body was much revised with dual round headlamps on each side and a smoother line at the front.

Daimler continued to exist as a marque with this the Double-Six using the V-12 engine. A Jaguar by any other name, it kept its individual nature by suitable changes to the trim and fittings, celebrating 100 years of existence in 1996.

One of the modern models was this XJ Executive of 1996 fitted with the optional alloy wheels. By then the firm had long since overcome its quality control build problems and its models were squarely aimed at the sophisticated and performance markets.

In 1996 Daimler unveiled the Corsica concept car as a mark of their centenary and to pay tribute to their place as Britain's oldest car maker. It was built to enhance their name for luxury, elegance and performance using a saloon car floorpan as the basis. With a drop-head coupé, two-door, four-seater body it was a one-off, not intended for production.

Late in 1996 the firm launched the XK8 in coupé and convertible forms, both powered by the 4.0-litre, 32-valve V-8 engine with twin camshafts for each cylinder bank, this driving a five-speed automatic transmission. Built for the sports car market in the XK tradition, both models incorporated all the modern refinements in all areas for a car of the 21st century.

Late in 1998 the new S-type made its debut at the British Motor Show to take the firm back to the compact saloon market of the old Mk II. Powered by either a 3.0-litre V-6 or 4.0-litre V-8 engine, the new car embodied all the refinements needed to take it into the 21st century while retaining some elements of the style of the past. It carried on the heritage left by Bill Lyons in a fine way and stole the show, just as his models had done so often in the past.

INDEX